# Where Ca a Hippo Hide?

Written by Emily Beth Gerard
Illustrated by Benrei Huang

Hannah wants to hide.

Hippo wants to hide, too.

Hannah hides behind the house.

4

Hippo can't hide behind the house.

Hannah hides behind the horse.

Hippo can't hide behind the horse.

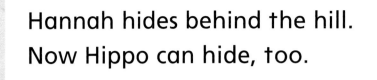

Hannah hides behind the hill.
Now Hippo can hide, too.